Bizjets

Bizjets

EXECUTIVE JETS IN COLOUR

Thomas Manser and Rolf Kurz

Airlife
England

Dedication

Bizjets is dedicated to all those with dirty hands from spilled oil and grey hair from dozens of hours overtime – those who keep bizjets in the air.

Acknowledgements

Bizjets would not have been possible without the help of Mary and Walter Steinegger. Many thanks also to Victoria Zweidler-Rich, Jennifer Flatz and Cheri Lawry who helped improve the text. We would also like to thank Markus Moser who made many suggestions and many others who have supported this project.

First published in the UK in 1999
by Airlife Publishing Ltd

British Library Cataloguing-in-Publication Data
A catalogue record for this book
is available from the British Library

ISBN 1 84037 090 4

Printed in Singapore.

Airlife Publishing Ltd

101 Longdon Road, Shrewsbury, SY3 9EB, England
E-mail: airlife@airlifebooks.com
Website: www.airlifebooks.com

Contents

Introduction

Our fascination with bizjets started a few years ago when we first met each other whilst both employed as aircraft mechanics. We had both been aviation photographers for a long time and aircraft enthusiasts since childhood. It took a while for our love of business jets to develop, but the longer we spent at our maintenance facility and on the tarmac at Zürich-Kloten Airport, the more our fascination with bizjets grew. Nearly every day we discovered new differences between types, series and serial numbers. We saw private 707s, camouflaged military bizjets, statesmen and pop stars disembarking their Gulfstreams, the arrival of ambulance flights and a surprising number of different aircraft types and series. We soon discovered how little aircraft enthusiasts know about the deliberately inconspicuous operations of business jets and therefore decided to compile this book.

The beginnings of business aviation lie in September 1957 when the Lockheed Model 329 made its first flight, followed by the North American NA-246 1958. Both aircraft had been built to meet military requirements for a utility transport and training aircraft and became the famous Jetstar and Sabreliner. At that point aircraft manufacturers did not envisage a large civilian market and nobody could predict that thousands of civilian jets would be sold in the near future. The military orders for these jets were their guarantee of success. After the groundwork had been laid to fulfil military orders, civil aviation also had a new sort of aircraft – the business jet. The T-39 Sabreliner was sold in large quantities to the USAF. In contrast the Jetstar had to find civilian customers after the first few military orders. The de Havilland DH 125 was similarly boosted by an early military order but was largely built for the civilian market.

Although at the start of the bizjet age there were few types available, the range soon expanded. New jets were simply the logical conclusion of developing and improving previous types. The engineers encountered a lot of new problems at first. A bizjet should have approximately the same cruising speed and altitude as an airliner, so the wings should be thin with laminar aerofoils and the engines should be powerful. However, throughout the sixties the engines were comparatively weak (although noisy and thirsty) and aerofoils couldn't be calculated with the aid of high performance computers. Bizjets were also required to use small airfields. This meant large wingspans but large wings produce a lot of drag so the jets would have the slow cruising speed of DC-4s. Engineers then designed lift-increasing devices such as double-slotted flaps and slats to shorten take-offs. At that time Kevlar composites were not yet available and the weight of aircraft rapidly increased. To keep the wingload low they had to reduce weight elsewhere, so fuel capacity decreased. Early bizjets suffered from poor range which was compounded by additional external fuel tanks as on the Jetstar. Building a 'mini-airliner' or business jet was therefore a real challenge and today's manufacturers have profited from the pioneers' efforts.

In the sixties Learjet and Gulfstream entered the business jet market. In Europe Dassault and Hawker Siddeley also started to build jets. Bill Lear sent one of his Learjet 24s around the globe and set eighteen world records. He was a master of public relations and used every opportunity to publicise his Learjet, perhaps benefiting other manufacturers in the process. Soon Learjets were established as the leading business jets and even some early accidents did not hinder their success. People started to call any bizjet a 'Learjet'. Unfortunately, not every aircraft builder was as successful as Lear or Dassault. There were also failures such as the Aérospatiale Corvette, the German HFB 320 and the Italian Piaggio PD 808. Other companies such as Cessna, Beechcraft and Canadair found their niches in the market and survived despite increasingly stiff competition.

The need has arisen for a small jet for the executive who has to travel quickly within a continent and independently of an airline schedule. The aircraft must have a high cruising speed, be affordable to maintain and readily available. For those who need to travel worldwide, the manufacturers have created the king-size inter-continental bizjet. Not only a means of transport which travels faster and on higher airways to avoid the congestion of slower airliners, these aircraft are used as flying offices and are equipped with satellite communication, fax, telex, and personal computers. The over-stressed executive can also rest in the onboard bedroom before he goes into the conference room to close an important deal.

In order to transport customers to a desired destination punctually, today's bizjets are equipped with navigational tools and safety systems which are often more advanced than those of airliners. An autopilot equipped with a flight management system (FMS) and GPS is no longer unique. The FMS calculates flight time, distance, altitude, alternative airports, fuel consumption and much more. To keep the airspace free and avoid near misses, collision warning systems have become standard. For those who fear corporate spies or even violent competitors there is an anti-terrorist system available which registers every removal or opening of access panels on the ground and even indicates if somebody has put his hand into the landing gear wheel well. The world of business and finance can change quickly, and people have to be flexible. A company simply cannot afford a transaction or an important deal to be delayed.

There have always been those who can afford a little bit more. These people convert airliners such as Boeing 727s into flying penthouses. In the former Soviet Union large aircraft are flown as bizjets, but the lack of suitable aircraft there has forced companies to use slightly old-fashioned Yaks and Tupolevs.

With the aid of a bizjet a manager can travel from Southampton to Karlsruhe, Germany, in approximately seventy minutes. Without the bizjet he has to check-in at Southampton Airport an hour before departure. He then flies in a narrow commuter aircraft to London-Heathrow where he has to wait for the delayed departure of the airliner to take him to Stuttgart. When he finally leaves Customs and baggage reclaim, he has to travel by train or organise a limousine to take him to Karlsruhe. Business without bizjets is unthinkable today.

What lies in the future? Unlike thirty years ago, it is difficult to find a niche in the market. Aircraft manufacturers try to design jets which meet different requirements – jets for every class of business. For example, Cessna currently offers six different-sized jets and has sold over 2500. In these difficult times companies try to be innovative. In France engineers have started to design a supersonic bizjet. A similar design also exists by Sukhoi, but so far the Russians have only successfully built mock-ups. Nevertheless, development continues and hopefully the future will bring some interesting designs which can be featured in *Bizjets Vol 2*.

Bestsellers:
The Citation 500 series

Above: In 1992 the Dutch carrier KLM operated four Citation 500s. PH-CTE is a frequent visitor at Zürich Airport. Although the aircraft was built as construction number 167 and therefore is quite old, it is equipped with modern avionics which are comparable to those of a large airliner. One of the few handling differences compared to say a Boeing 737 is the absence of thrust reversers. Note the old-style wing tips which identify the aircraft as a Citation 500.

Above: Cessna Citation I HB-VIC, c/n 501-0098, is about to undergo extensive maintenance and receive a fresh coat of paint. The upper and lower engine cowlings are removed in order to facilitate the detection of any bleed air, fuel or oil leaks at the earliest stage of maintenance.

Right: HB-VIC was photographed again in March 1995 with a new coat of paint and polished aluminium windshield retainers. From leaving the Wichita production line in 1978 to 22 March 1995, this aircraft amassed 6383 flight hours and 6105 landings. Following quality maintenance, this aircraft was ready to provide further service.

8

Above: Like many of his former colleagues, ex-Formula I driver Thierry Boutsen is a proud owner of a business jet. This club of globe-trotters appreciate the advantages of luxury travel and saving time. His Citation I, c/n 501-0107, bears a 3A registration from the tax paradise Monaco. The black radome is quite unusual on Citations.

Above: This Cessna, c/n 501-0161, is no average Citation I. Mexican-registered XB-FXO is special in two ways. First, it is an Eagle modification. Sierra Industries Inc. in Uvalde, Texas, offers this modification by redesigning the wing fuel tanks to increase the aircraft's total fuel capacity to 689 gallons usable fuel instead of 564 gallons. The thicker wing is clearly visible. Second, this Citation I Eagle is equipped with rarely seen silver-coloured high speed de-ice boots on the wings and empennage.

Right: N91WZ, a Model 501 Citation I, c/n 501-0132, was photographed shortly before engine start-up in November 1994. The US registration is a little misleading, as this aircraft is owned by Prince Georg of Waldburg-Zeil and is based in Leutkirch-Unterzeil, Germany.

Below: N900SE, c/n 551-0016, started its life as a Citation II, c/n 550-0338. Cessna later decreased the maximum permissible take-off weight of this aircraft and returned it to service as a Model 551. In some countries, including the USA, it is placed in another aircraft category, making it possible to operate it as a single pilot aircraft.

Above: OE-GIN, the sixty-ninth Model 550 to be built, is operated by Amadeus Air based in Vienna. In 1993 this Citation II appeared as a member of the United Nations' air fleet. During the UN missions the aircraft saw many countries where it had to prove itself on poorly equipped airfields. However, OE-GIN managed this challenge without any major problems.

Opposite above: Production of the Citation II was discontinued with the introduction of the Citation SII in 1984. Nevertheless, most customers didn't like the SII and continued to ask for newly-built Citation IIs. Cessna therefore reopened the Citation II production line in 1987 with c/n 550-0550. Newly-built Citation IIs were then called Citation II Classics like OY-RDD, c/n 550-0621, seen here.

Opposite below: At the end of January 1995, HB-VIS left Pilatus Aircraft Ltd's paint hangar in Stans/Switzerland wearing this ingenious paint scheme. Eight seats are available for business travellers in this Citation II, c/n 550-0447, owned by Cat Aviation. This Zürich-based company also owns a second bizjet, a BAe 125-800 Hawker.

Above: PT-LLU is one of two Citation IIs operated by Turbo Taxi Aereo based in Rio de Janeiro. The aircraft was photographed whilst awaiting its preflight check on the ramp at Wichita, Kansas, before its long flight back to Brazil. The electrically operated flaps can be seen in their landing position. The deflection, together with the use of speed brakes and thrust reversers, enables the aircraft to use short strips, which are normally reserved for propeller aircraft.

Above: Cessna offered the option to modify Citations with a wide cargo door. The wider opening plus the absence of the normally laterally fastened entrance door is especially helpful for loading and unloading stretchers for ambulance flights. N30CX, the seventh Citation SII built, has been modified.

Below: Citation V TC-LAB, c/n 560-0216, is one of two identical-looking Turkish aircraft illustrated in this photograph taken in July 1996. Citation V is easily distinguished from the Citation II as it has an additional cabin window.

Opposite above: Australian-registered VH-FHJ, c/n 560-0278, is an example of one of Cessna's most popular models. At the end of 1997, a second-hand Citation V Ultra like this one built in 1994, was worth between five to six million US Dollars, nearly the same price as a new one. At the same time only three Citation V Ultras of a similar age were even up for sale – an indication of satisfied customers.

Opposite below: With its engine cowlings removed and landing lights on, S5-BAC appears to be posing for the camera. This Citation II, c/n 550-0480, is operated by the Slovenian company SMELT, and was one of the last Citation IIs to be built with a pneumatically controlled Garrett AIResearch air cycle machine. All Citation IIs from c/n 550-0485 on are equipped with electrically controlled Hamilton Standard ACM.

Below: The Cessna S550 Citation SII is unique in the Cessna 500 series. It is the only model not equipped with black rubber de-ice boots. A TKS ethylene glycol wing and tail anti-icing system is used instead. Out of 160 Citation SIIs built, some twenty are flown by EJI Net Jets based in Columbus, Ohio. This Portuguese-registered Cessna, c/n S550-0032, is owned by Net Jets Europe based in Zürich.

Mid-size made in Wichita: The 650s

Above: Toprak Air based in Istanbul operates TC-TOP, a Model 650 Citation III. Before being sold to Turkey it was one of Honeywell's bizjets. The avionics company changed the cockpit layout and used the aircraft as a special avionics demonstrator. The new arrangement of instruments and an additional INS (Inertial Navigation System) were never put into production by Cessna, so TC-TOP remains a 'prototype'.

Above: Formerly registered EC-EAS and owned by Gestair Executive Jet SA, this aircraft was photographed in Zürich. It had just been sold to Automotive Management Services Inc. and was awaiting its delivery flight to Daytona Beach, Florida. A sticker currently covers the old registration of this Citation III, but both the registration and Spanish flag will be removed by a proper paint job in the USA.

Right: This Citation III, c/n 650-0043, is one of three aircraft flying worldwide with toy manufacturer LEGO-Systems A/S based in Billund, Denmark. The Citation III is no longer produced. Its successors the VI and VII differ only in their engines, avionics and cabin interiors. From the outside they can hardly be distinguished from the Citation III.

20

Above: C-FIMO, c/n 65, was photographed in front of the fuel station at
Cessna's maintenance centre at Wichita
minus its flight controls and both
engines, which were probably taken
away to be overhauled. The TFE731
engine of the Model 650 is held in
place by only four bolts. Two of the
bolts have to carry the weight of the
engine and the power of the thrust,
whilst the other two bolts keep the
engine aligned with the pylon. Note the
hook on top of the vertical stabiliser
which indicates the tailplane will soon
be removed. All early Model 650s had
to undergo this procedure to reinforce
the stabiliser's ribs and protect them
against cracks.

Above: Citation VII N737CC was photographed in June 1994 whilst still owned by Cessna. Shortly afterwards, c/n 650-7037 was transferred to the Textron Corporation registered as N95TX. What is unusual is that Cessna is owned by the Textron Corporation.

Right: Zürich-based HB-VLP is operated by Jet Aviation Business Jets on behalf of General Motors. This Citation VII, c/n 650-7064, is quite new and the only aircraft of its type in the Swiss register. The Fowler flaps are in their landing position (the gap allows the air to keep a laminar flow along the flaps) whilst the elevator is trimmed nose-up.

Cessna's flying testbeds

Above: From 1992 Cessna used N650 as a testbed for the Citation X powerplant, the Allison AE3007C. The TFE731 engine is still installed on the left-hand side. With time N650 was brought up to Citation VII standard. It received the somewhat strange serial number 697. Note the anti-spin drag chute on the tail and the long nose probe.

Above: N501CC is a Citation I which was used by Cessna to test the systems of the CitationJet. Built as c/n 670 it is now c/n 701. In 1994 the aircraft was fitted with one JT15D and one Williams FJ44 engine.

Below: JPATS contestant N526JT was given the designation Model 526 by Cessna. It was photographed whilst still unpainted, taxying across Cessna's maintenance area at Wichita Airport. The Model 526, which lost the JPATS competition against the Raytheon/Pilatus T-6A, is comprised of many CitationJet parts. The landing gear, wings, horizontal stabiliser and engines, including thrust attenuators, were taken nearly unmodified from the Model 525.

Babyjet: The 525

Above: N532CJ is CitationJet c/n 525-0032. When photographed at McConnell AFB the Model 525 was still owned by Cessna's demonstrators. In this photograph it is clearly visible that the single-piece wing is positioned below the fuselage to maintain the same height for the full length of the cabin. Another difference to the CitationJet's predecessor, the Model 500, is the relocation of the emergency exit. It does not contain a window and is visible next to the engine inlet.

Above: N594JB, a brand-new CitationJet, is being prepared for a test flight prior to delivery. Look closely at the ice protection systems of the Model 525. The engine inlets and wing leading edges are heated by bleed air whilst the horizontal stabiliser is equipped with the good old de-ice boot. The vertical stabiliser does not have any de-ice equipment. The white stripes visible on the radome are lightning diverters.

Above: Cessna's CitationJet is easy to fly, able to operate from short runways, fuel efficient, quiet and approximately the same price as a turboprop. Operating costs are less than that of turboprops, and there are no comparable new jets produced by rival manufacturers. It is therefore no surprise that Cessna delivered 250 CitiationJets from April 1993 to June 1998. D-IHHS, c/n 525-0082, belongs to the steadily expanding German CitationJet fleet.

Above: It took over twenty years before some Citations started to leave Cessna's paint hangars without the traditional and somewhat boring fuselage striping. Demonstrators tended to receive more modern paint schemes such as the first Citation V Ultra or this CitationJet, c/n 525-0121, which was sold to Rubi Air based in Istanbul. Some customers repainted their Citations with this new type of abstract striping design. Even today, new Citations still leave Cessna facilities in Wichita with the timeless striping.

The American way of flying: Learjets

Above: Thoroughly polished and pampered, N701SC is always kept in excellent condition. Built in 1971 as Learjet 24D c/n 24D-235, it is faster than all later built Learjet models and together with the Concorde was one of the first civilian aircraft certified for flights up to 51,000 feet. N701SC is an extended range conversion of the Learjet 24 and designated Learjet 24XR.

29

Below: When this photograph was taken in March 1991, one and a half years after Germany's reunification, Learjet 35A c/n 35A-174 still flew with the US registration N310TA. The German ambulance organisation DRF acquired this N-registration to perform ambulance transports from and to West Berlin when West German-registered aircraft were forbidden to fly over East German territory.

Opposite above: Like the Learjet 23 and 24, the Model 25 is powered by sleek and noisy General Electric CJ610 turbojet engines. The fuselage, however, has been stretched by 52 inches to accommodate two additional seats and more fuel. MAC-Aviation's Learjet 25B, based in Zaragoza, Spain, made its last landing at Northolt AB, England, on 13 August 1996 when it overshot the runway and crashed into a Transit van on the A40 highway. This picture was taken in January 1994. Note the serial number on the tailfin.

Opposite below: Learjet 35A HB-VHR is owned by Jet Service AG, based in Zürich, and was photographed in January 1992. Learjet's original plan was to build a more fuel efficient model, so the company intended to re-engine the turbojet-powered Learjet 25 with new Garrett TFE731-2 turbofans. The Learjet 26 was announced in 1969 but weight and balance problems forced Learjet to stretch the fuselage and extend the wing. The result was much better than the original idea and became the Learjet 35.

Above: Formerly registered YU-BOL and owned by the Slovenian Government, this aircraft was photographed in Zürich-Kloten in November 1993. This Learjet 35A was damaged when Ljubljana Airport was attacked in Yugoslavia's civil war. In 1991 it was flown to Nürnberg, Germany, where Aero Dienst Nürnberg replaced the whole vertical stabiliser and the rudder. It returned to service with the Slovenian Government, but operated from Klagenfurt, Austria, until Ljubljana was safe again.

Above: D-COCO, a Learjet 35A, was photographed in 1992 whilst parked near runway 28 at Zürich-Kloten Airport. This aircraft was operated by Aero Dienst Nürnberg and had a tragic demise on 7 June 1993 when it crashed shortly after take-off from Köln-Bonn Airport in Germany. All four people on board were killed.

Below: Learjet 35A SX-BNT, c/n 35A-228, of Aegean Aviation based in Athens is one of only a few Greek business jets. Aegean Aviation has owned this Learjet since February 1995 and received a Learjet 55 in December 1995. Although the Greek business jet fleet seems very small, there are several aircraft with Greek owners in countries such as Bermuda and the United States.

Opposite below: Eye-catching paint schemes are too rare in business aviation. Learjet 55 D-CCON, c/n 55-098, owned by the charter operator Aero Continentale/Primair based in Munich is one of twelve Learjet 55s registered in Germany.

Opposite above: N80LJ displays the sleek lines of the Lear 31 in the evening sun at Bombardier's Wichita base. Until the Learjet 45's development, the company built its jets with only two types of fuselage. The Lear 31 is equipped with the narrow-type fuselage and is one of the fastest jets in its class.

Below: This Altenrhein-based Learjet 60, c/n 60-010, was bought by Satronic AG shortly after former Formula I champion Niki Lauda demonstrated his own Lear 60 in Altenrhein. The enthusiasm of the new owner soon ended, when it was realised that Altenrhein's runway was too short for a fully loaded commercially certified Lear 60 (in case of an aborted take-off). HB-VLU was photographed on 11 September 1996 in Zürich following licensing procedures with the Swiss Aviation Authorities. It was sold again about one year later.

Opposite above: Learjet 55 VR-BQF, c/n 55-039, is registered in Bermuda and was photographed in August 1996. The midsize jet features a newly developed extended wing with winglets and a longer and wider fuselage than its predecessor the Learjet 35.

Opposite below: Each Learjet 60 Pratt & Whitney PW305 engine delivers 4600 lb thrust. The same engine type is also installed on Raytheon's Hawker 1000. An auxiliary power unit (APU) used to supply electric power before the engines are started is optional. Learjet 60 HB-VKI does not have an APU and normally uses the right-hand engine to provide air conditioning until the passengers are seated.

Above: The typical thin Learjet wing was based on the design of the Swiss P-16 fighter-bomber. Today's Learjet wings have been completely redesigned and no longer have anything in common with any fighter. Note the aerodynamically redesigned wing-to-fuselage fairing of the Learjet 60, made possible with NASA computer software. Privately owned Learjet 60 PT-OVI, c/n 60-008, is registered in Brazil.

Right: Bill Lear's first business jet, the Model 23, became so popular that until recently many people called any small bizjet a Learjet. The Learjet 23 and the early Learjet 24 are easily recognised by the tailfin bullet and large cabin windows. The sixth Learjet 23 off the assembly line, N505PF has been removed from service and is preserved at the Kansas Aviation Museum.

Five o'clock tea in the jet:
The HS series

Above: Hawker 125 F-BSIM, c/n 25130, is a Series 3B aircraft. Series 1 and Series 1A/B aircraft were equipped with RR Viper 520/521 engines. Series 3A/B Hawkers featured already more improved aircraft systems, including RR Viper 522 engines with 240 lb more thrust than the Viper 521. Series 3A/B became the last Hawker series without a ventral fin or a fuel tank located underneath the rear fuselage.

Above: This Hawker 125-600B, c/n 256035, was owned by the Hawker engine supplier Rolls-Royce. While many owners equipped their Model 600s with Garrett engines, G-BETV still contains all-British parts including the Viper engines. However, the success of the RR Viper engine ended with the first stretched version of the Hawker 125.

Above: Hawker 125-700 G-IECL, seen here in service with Stansted UK-based Inflite Executive Charter Ltd, was the second Hawker 700, c/n 257002, off the production line. It was also the first 700 with US standard outfitting. Every Hawker conforming to this US standard is called an A-model and has a US reference number (NA0201).

Left: This Nigerian Government Hawker 125-700B, c/n 257160, with its highly visible markings is waiting for a pair of overhauled Garrett TFE731-3R-1H engines.

Below: During tightly-planned business trips bizjets don't stay on the ground for long because time is money. With chocks removed, the crew already on board and the stairs in place, C-FFAB waits for the big boss. This Hawker BAe 125-700A (NA0222) is painted in a typical white scheme. Most businessmen want to travel inconspicuously.

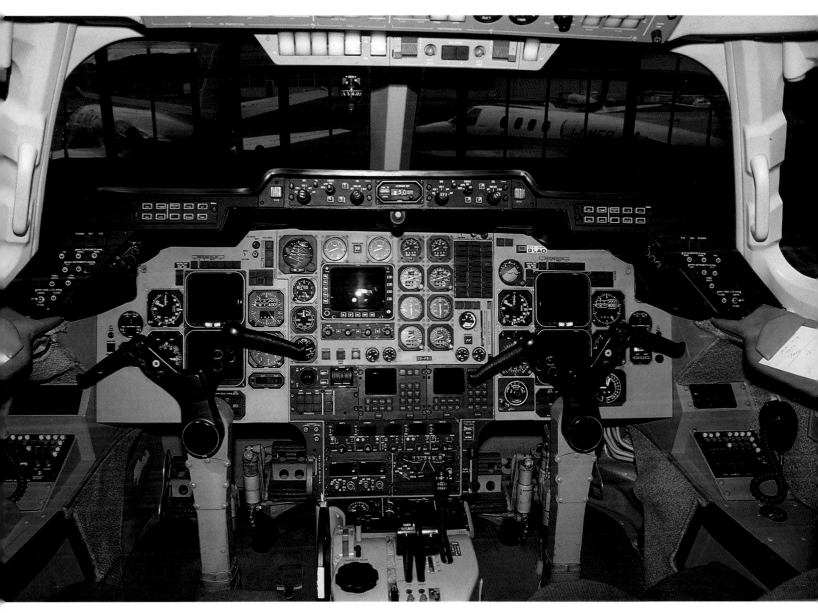

Above: A mix of new EFIS (Electronic Flight Instrument System) displays and common round pointer instruments can be found in the cockpit of a BAe 125-800B. This is ZS-FSI owned by Osprey Aerospace based in Johannesburg, South Africa. The main flight instruments are combined in groups in front of the characteristic 'bicycle handlebars' whilst the centre panel displays the big weather radar screen and the engine instruments. Standby flight instruments can also be seen in the centre panel. The lower is fitted with the autopilot controls, flight management system and communication and radio navigation equipment. The engine controls, flap handle and trims are just visible on the centre pedestal. Whilst the Series 800 shows a modern pilot's working place, the cockpit layout of the first DH 125 was improvised and contained many instruments from the de Havilland Comet as there was not any suitable equipment available.

Above: Registered HB-VHU, this BAe 125-800A, c/n 258152, is one of two Rabbit Air Hawkers. It was photographed in May 1991 whilst approaching runway 14 of its homebase at Zürich-Kloten Airport.

Opposite above: Six BAe C-29A flight-checking aircraft are used by the FAA to check and calibrate ground-installed navigation and landing aids. N98 is a former US Air Force aircraft with the military serial number 88-0273. It is based on the BAe 125-800 and was stopped on 22 August 1995 for maintenance in Zürich.

Opposite below: For some reason, some people do not believe that flying a Hawker (in this case a BAe 125-800A) is safe enough. When photographed in January 1994, the Italian registered I-CASG, c/n 258033, was protected by an expensive sensor system, which monitored all aircraft access panels and movements in the wheel well area whilst the aircraft was parked. Note the arched-type windshield.

Above: VR-CPT is the second Hawker 1000 with a real 1000 serial number, c/n 259004. The numbers 259001 and 259002 were not used. The Hawker 1000 is a greatly-improved BAe 125-800, easily identified by the stretched fuselage, an additional window and the new Pratt & Whitney 305 engines. Executive Jet Aviation, based in Columbus, Ohio, operates the most Hawker 1000s with its 'Net Jets' ownership programme. VR-CPT is owned by Remo Investments in Biggin Hill.

En français: Falcons

Above: Although the Falcon 10 looks a little old-fashioned in today's bizjet world, it is still one of the fastest jets of its class. This aircraft, c/n 88, is owned by Regourd Aviation based in Paris-Le Bourget. Unlike many other jets of the same size, the Falcon 10 is fitted with leading edge slats which allow short take-offs and a high level of manoeuvrability. These attributes can be traced back to the Falcon 10's 'uncle', the Mystère IV fighter.

Left: 9A-CRL, the Falcon 10 operated by Air Exclusive, joined the small Croatian business jet scene shortly after the national registration prefix was changed from RC to 9A. A year after its visit to Zürich in 1996, the Falcon disappeared from the register.

Below: Nearly twenty Falcons are operated by Iran Asseman Airlines and the Iranian Islamic Revolutionary Forces. Without exception they need special permission to touch down on Swiss territories. In this case Falcon 20E EP-FIF, c/n 320, was operating an ambulance flight to Zürich-Kloten. Whether the VIPs onboard this aircraft really visited the doctor is not known. The Falcon 20E was photographed on 8 May 1996 and left for Istanbul, Turkey, the same day.

Above: OY-BDS is the sole Falcon 20C of the Danish trading company Danfoss. Flight operations of this aircraft are carried out by Air Alsie. Although OY-BDS bears the designation '20C', Dassault never built an official 'C' model. The 'D' model was introduced after the basic model Falcon 20 or Mystère 20. OY-BDS, c/n 180, is a basic Falcon 20 equipped with more powerful engines.

Below: One of the World Economic Forum's regular visitors is Falcon 50 YV-452CP, owned by Maraves SA based in Caracas, Venezuela. The fourth Falcon 50 to be built, it left the Dassault plant in 1979. At the time *Spirit of Mérignac* was unpainted and demonstrated long-range flights in the USA.

Below: More than 60 per cent of all business jets are registered in the United States. This doesn't mean that these N-registered aircraft are all operated in the USA or by Americans. However, it is evident that bizjet manufacturers have to be successful in the US market to survive. This is the case for Dassault and its Falcons. This Falcon 50 was photographed catching the last rays of sunshine on a summer day in 1996.

Below: PH-ILR was built as c/n 15 and is one of two Falcon 50s owned by Philips, based in Eindhoven, Netherlands. The Falcon 50 has much in common with the Falcon 20 (it is sometimes called a three-engined Falcon 20), but has a new wing and was designed to be able to cross the American continent non-stop.

Opposite above: HB-IAM started service with IBM-Switzerland in August 1986. For more than ten years this Falcon 50 took Switzerland-based executives to worldwide destinations. IBM-France then used c/n 164, registered as N164MA, from Paris-Le Bourget.

Opposite below: Despite single point pressure refuelling, refuelling a Falcon 50 is time-consuming. For flights up to 3500 nm, over 2315 gallons of Jet A1 kerosene has to be taken onboard. The Mexican flag is present under the cockpit window of Mexico City-based XA-RVV.

Above: Although Hawkers and Citations owned by the Nigerian Government sometimes visit maintenance facilities in Zürich-Kloten, Falcon 900 5N-FGO was a welcome ordinary visitor in February 1995. It is not only the Nigerian Government which trusts the triple-engined Falcon 900. It has proved popular with a number of governments and air forces, particularly because of its cabin space and transcontinental range.

Below: Charter operator Aeroleasing SA based in Geneva is a regular customer of Dassault Falcons. This Falcon 900, c/n 35, belongs to its fleet, and is seen here with its entrance and baggage doors open, ready for service.

Below: This Kuala Lumpur-based Falcon 900 is a Malaysian Government executive jet and is actually a Falcon 900B. The Falcon 900B uses Allied Signal (former Garrett) TFE731-5B turbofans, which provide improved field performance, climb and range. 9M-BAB is equipped with satellite communication, indicated by the square-shaped antenna just behind the entrance door.

Right: This shot of N5733 clearly shows the thrust reverser which is only fitted to engine number two. This Falcon 900, c/n 39, is a member of the Falcon fleet owned by Enron Corporation based in Houston, Texas. Unusually the registration, N5733, was taken over from a Falcon 50 and is used here for a second time by Enron.

Below: Falcon 2000 number 6, was photographed in dry conditions on 17 September 1995. The widebody fuselage of this aircraft is based on the Falcon 900, but is shorter. Closing the gap between the Falcon 50 and Falcon 900, the 2000 offers cheaper operating costs, made possible by its two-engine concept and use of advanced technology. Its size and performance puts it in direct competition with another comfortable widebody, Bombardier's Challenger.

Below: An all-white Falcon 900B, registered VP-BJA, was photographed on final approach to Zürich's runway 14. Jacobs' aircraft was formerly registered VR-BJA. The nationality mark had to be changed from 1 July 1997 to VP-B, as the ITU re-allocated the VR-A to VR-Q series to China. A satcom antenna can be discerned as a 'patch' on the forward upper fuselage.

Little widebodies: Challengers

Above: This CL-600S is one of 76 Challengers which have been retrofitted with winglets. Together with the deer head, the gold and orange paint scheme indicates that HB-ILH is a member of Jet Aviation's large bizjet fleet. The colours were chosen by Mr Hirschmann senior, the late owner of the company. All CL-600s are equipped with Lycoming ALF502 engines.

Below: Crossing the Atlantic Ocean was no problem for N439CL, which is owned by Electronic Data Systems Corp based in Dallas, Texas. It is a Challenger 601-3A but has been upgraded to 3R standard by the addition of an extended tailcone fuel tank which increases the range to more than 3500 nm. The 3A version Challengers were the first models with 'glass' cockpits and fully integrated digital flight guidance and flight management systems. The General Electric engines, now standard on all Challengers, are able to maintain their maximum thrust up to 21°C.

Opposite above: Before VR-CHK found its way to the Cayman Islands' register the Challenger 601-3A was operated by Thai Airways. The large patch next to the cabin door indicates that the jet is fitted with a satcom system which enables passengers to communicate worldwide.

Opposite below: VR-BNG was photographed on a cold winter morning in Zürich. This Challenger 601-3A is operated by Jet Aviation Business Jets but owned by the Turkish television company Intelstar. More than eighty Challenger 3As are known to be equipped with the extended tailcone which houses a fuel tank and increases the gross weight by 500 lb.

Above: N39CD was photographed in full Global Aviation colours. It is a Challenger 601-1A, the first production version equipped with CF34 engines. After sixty-six 601-1As were built, Bombardier produced the 3A equipped with modernised avionics and engines. Singapore-based Global Aviation offers its customers an increasingly popular jet-sharing scheme. Individual people or companies can buy 'part' of a bizjet and therefore have the right to use the aircraft for a certain number of hours per year. Maintenance and operating costs are shared. This is a new way of 'owning' a jet without incurring costs when the aircraft is on the ground.

Faster, higher, further: Gulfstreams

Above: This Moroccan Gulfstream II TT has a large wing fence and vortex generators in front of the ailerons, the usual expedients used to optimise aerodynamics. Powered by two Rolls-Royce Spey engines, each producing 11,400 lb thrust, it would be able to fly with any type of wing.

Left: Chrysler Pentastar is the flight department of the Chrysler Corporation and responsible for company-owned aircraft such as this Gulfstream II TT. Their facilities at Oakland-Pontiac Airport include a service centre authorised by Gulfstream Aerospace, where they also perform aircraft maintenance and overhauls for other customers. N807CC carries a rarely seen stinger antenna on its tail, probably an HF antenna.

Below: Gulfstream IIB VR-BND is a Gulfstream II retrofitted with a Gulfstream III wing. Serial number 199 was built in 1977 and also has a G III radome installed. At a price that is a minimum of two-thirds that of its nearest competitor (the G III), the ability to fly 3700 nautical miles made many Gulfstream owners convert their aircraft into G IIBs instead of buying new Gulfstream IIIs.

Above: Gulfstream Parke Aviation Corporation's Gulfstream III is seen here at Zürich Airport before its departure to New York. Like many Gulfstream IIIs N270MC's engines are fitted with hush kits to comply with today's noise restriction laws. In order to reduce wake turbulence, the wing is displaying its typical winglets. Vortex generators are placed on top of the wing as more turbulence is required near the ailerons.

Below: Turkey received this Gulfstream IV with the registration TC-ANA. ANA means mother and stood for Anavatan Partisi (Motherland Party), the party of President Turgut Ozal. After a change of government the new president, Süleyman Demirel, changed ANA to ATA. ATA stands for Mustafa Kemal Atatürk, the founder of modern Turkey.

Opposite above: King Hussein bin Talal of Jordan was a pilot and aircraft enthusiast, who sometimes insisted on flying government aircraft himself. Two Gulfstream IIIs, c/n 467 and 469, were delivered to join his fleet. JY-HZH, c/n 469, displays a noble colour scheme with golden titles and cheatline.

Opposite below: Gulfstream III 5X-UOI is the only business jet in Uganda's aircraft register and also the government's aircraft. It was photographed at Zürich-Kloten on 27 January 1995.

Left: *The Spirit of Savannah*, one of the first Gulfstream IVSPs, is used as a demonstrator for the Gulfstream Aerospace Corporation. Equipped with the same Rolls-Royce Tay engines as the Fokker 100 but with 23,000 lb less take-off weight, N485GA can be described as slightly overpowered. The two windows outlined in green are the emergency exits.

Below: 9M-TRI, a Gulfstream IVSP operated by MHS Aviation, based in Kuala Lumpur, was photographed shortly after its arrival in Zürich. The letters TRI stand for 'Technology Resources Industry'. As soon as the engines are shut down the aircraft is surrounded by Jet Aviation servicing and VIP cars.

Made in Israel: IAI birds

Above: Westwind N455S is prepared for departure at Zürich Airport's Sector 1. The aircraft was on its way to the United States when it stopped at Zürich for a quick repair on its brakes.

Above: Here is another bizjet in airline colours. SE-DLL of Air Sweden (now West Air Sweden) is used for executive transport. The Westwind is the result of modifying the old-fashioned bizprop Twin Commander. Because the forward part of the cabin is so far from the centre of gravity, a single passenger is requested to take a seat in the back!

Left: This is N1124N, the Westwind II operated by Semitool Inc. The Model II is easily recognised by the large winglets on the tiptanks. Only the fuselage, 'hanging' between the wings near the ground, is a reminder of the Westwind's 'grandfather', the Twin Commander.

Below: Demonstrating its large size in the evening sun, Astra 1125/N125GB is the executive transport of Kangra Group, based in Johannesburg. Although the Astra's fuselage and tail section are a reminder of its predecessor the Westwind, it is a completely new aircraft. The swept-wing design permits higher cruising speeds and the wing spar no longer crosses the cabin.

Above: There seems to be room for everybody in the corporate aviation business. Hundreds of small companies operating only one aircraft exist. One mini airline is Hannover-based Wiking Flight Service which has six employees (including the charming lady piloting the aircraft) and one IAI 1125 Astra SP. At the time this photograph was taken D-CCAT was also the only Astra SP in the German register. Powered by two reliable TFE731s and fitted with an APU, the Astra SP offers the same comfort and performance as any American bizjet in the same class.

Do you want more jets?

Above: The Morane MS 760 Paris 2B is rarely utilised as a bizjet. Only 165 Paris aircraft were built. N99HB was seen in Jet Aviation Zürich's hangar shortly before it was sold to the United States. The red band on the tailfin is a reminder that the vintage jet was once registered in Switzerland as HB-VEU. It also played a small role in the James Bond film *On Her Majesty's Secret Service*. Because of its noisy but weak Marboré engines the Paris wasn't allowed to perform many take-offs from Zürich.

Right: This isn't a Falcon 10 with tiptanks but one of forty Corvettes built by Aérospatiale in the early 1970s. F-BUQP is the first series production aircraft and is c/n 4 (the first prototype crashed in 1970, and c/n 2 and 3 were used for flight testing).

Below: Corvette 100 OY-SBT, c/n 33, is owned by Aalborg Air Taxi and was photographed whilst visiting Zürich. Although the Corvette was produced by the respected aircraft manufacturer Aérospatiale, it had little success compared with its counterparts the Citation 500 and Falcon 10. The major problem was the Pratt & Whitney strike in the early seventies. As a consequence of the strike several Corvette airframes were ready for delivery but had no engines.

Above: This Sabre 65 was photographed at the Mid-Continent Airport in Wichita, Kansas, in 1994. When this photograph was taken, N324ZR was for sale. The Sabre 65 prototype first flew in 1977. It was a modified version of the Sabre 60, but had a refined wing, and the General Electric engines were replaced by TFE731s. Note the sturdy landing gear which has its origins in military aviation.

Above: RST Aviation's OO-RSE was one of the last Sabre 65s to be built. It left the factory in 1981 and was purchased by the Antwerp-based company in 1993. Triangular windows were standard on all Sabres with the narrow-type fuselage.

Above: Arab Wings, a Royal Jordanian subsidiary, has two Sabreliner 75As in its small fleet. Manufactured in 1977, the Sabre 75A is the largest Sabreliner variant. An additional fuselage segment was constructed to allow passengers to stand upright in the cabin. North American kept the old-type wing of the Sabre 60 and installed General Electric CF700 aft fan engines.

Left: VR-CSM is a Jetstar which was converted to TFE731 engines. It displays the typical colours of Ashmawi Aviation based in Jeddah, Saudi Arabia. Since it is not unheard of for a car to collide with an aircraft, the pilot requested a warning light to be positioned beneath the nose.

Below: Flying Eagle Inc's Jetstar 731 was captured on film at Samedan in the heart of the Swiss Alps. The Jetstar 731 differs from the original Jetstar as it is powered by the popular TFE731 engine rather than the noisy JT12A. Another distinguishing feature is the relocation of the auxiliary fuel tanks beneath the wings. The Jetstar was one of the first widebody bizjets and was quite successful with more than 200 built. N333EC was the sixty-first Jetstar and had the serial number 5061.

Opposite above: A bizjet in full airline colours – Lithuanian Airlines has used Jetstar 731 LY-AMB for executive services since 1994. The Lithuanians quickly realised the advantages of using a western bizjet with common engines rather than for example a converted Yak-40. Affordable landing and noise charges was only one factor. Another factor was the availability of western spare parts which have become much easier to acquire in the former Soviet Union.

Opposite below: HZ-TNA, Prince Turki bin Nasser's Jetstar 731, was photographed shortly before departure at Zürich Airport. The open panel above the engine is the APU exhaust. It is usually started up about thirty minutes before take-off to cool the jet's cabin and to supply power to the avionics.

Left: Although the Jetstar is designed for high cruising altitudes with a pressurised cabin, the windows are rectangular and therefore require additional reinforcements along the window frames. N303LE is operated by Tarpon Resources Co based in Dallas, Texas, and is a Jetstar 731 which was originally fitted with Pratt & Whitney JT12A engines. All Jetstars are equipped with the all-moving tail unit to adjust the pitch trim.

Below: I-GIRL is a low serial number (A012SA) Mitsubishi MU-300 Diamond 1A which was assembled in San Angelo, Texas. This type made its first flight on August 1978. The improved Diamond 2 was later renamed Beechjet 400 when Beech acquired the manufacturing and developing rights. Diamond I-GIRL, built in 1981, uses Pratt & Whitney JT15D-4D engines without thrust reversers.

Eastern business

Above: RA02803, an HS 125-700B, was photographed during a maintenance stop at Zürich Airport. When photographed, it was owned by Ward Business Inc of Panama but operated by Avprom, based in Moscow. It takes a second glance to realise that one digit of the registration is painted as an 'O' instead of a zero.

Above: Before RA-02807 joined Moscow-based Meridian Air/Master Group, the BAe 125-800B was a member of Volkswagen's bizjet fleet.

Unlike the Ukraine, which started to change its registrations from digits into letters, Russia uses the five-digit code for western-built aircraft as well.

Because the aircraft's maintenance is performed by Zimex Aviation based in Switzerland, the Hawker is often seen in Zürich.

Below: CCCP-88279 is a Yak-40 which started its career with Aeroflot. In March 1991, when this photograph was taken, it was leased to Metro Cargo as a crew shuttle. After this Swiss/Russian cargo company collapsed, the aircraft was sold to Lietuva (now Air Lithuania) as LY-AAA and used as a VIP jet for Lithuania's government members.

Above: This Yak-40 was born to serve as a VIP jet when it was delivered to the Czechoslovakian Government in late 1974. However, in the 1990s OK-BYE was also used for scheduled flights by Tatra Air. In 1993 the Yak was handed over to the Slovak Government Flying Service with the prefix changed to 'OM'.

Below: Like OM-BYE, OM-BYL also started its career as a 'member' of the Czech Government. Built as a Yak-40K, it is equipped with a large cargo door on the left. Slovak and Swiss flags were shown during the Slovakian President's state visit to Switzerland.

Right: Now flying for Air Ukraine, Yak-40 UR-87566 appeared to be a private bizjet in 1994 when it was photographed. The aircraft was spotted in Zürich just before its departure to Naples. The owner was unknown.

Below: In order to meet western (or Saudi) bizjet standards, the Republic of Tatarstan uses Boeing 727-193 VR-CWC for executive transport. This Boeing is much older than many former Aeroflot Tupolevs and Yaks.

Left: The Turkmenistan Government displayed its Boeing 757-23A at the 1994 World Economic Forum in Switzerland shortly after delivery. EZ-A010 is used solely for VIP transport and has thirty-six seats.

Below: This Tu-134 was escorting a Su-30 and a Su-35 to Kauhava Air Base, Finland, in 1995. RA-65932 is not owned by either ROSSIYA or Aeroflot. It is the Sukhoi Design Bureau's crew support aircraft.

Below: In February 1994, just in time for the World Economic Forum, Kazakstan's government unveiled its Tu-154B-2 in a new paint scheme. Look closely at the titles and letters. The prefix 'UN' was added in Latin letters in late 1993, and the title 'Kazakhstan' is written in the old spelling (the 'h' was removed shortly afterwards) whilst the type designation behind the cockpit is still in Cyrillic letters. Note the long antenna used for satellite communication on top of the fuselage.

Opposite above: When we approached the Ukrainian Tu-134A-3 the navigator behind the glazed nose quickly covered his optical units and glared at us. In 1992 65556 did not have a prefix but a year later the prefix 'UR' was added.

Opposite below: This Tu-154B-2 is owned by Kazakstan's government and was photographed awaiting its passengers on the ramp at Zürich Airport, next to ROSSIYA's Tu-154M. In February 1993, 85464 was still wearing small Aeroflot titles below the cockpit but did not have a registration prefix. Officially this aircraft is owned by the Ministry of Defence together with a Tu-134.

Above: First added to some VIP aircraft, the grey painted tail has now become standard on most of Aeroflot's Tu-154s. When ROSSIYA's 85675 was painted in Shannon the prefix was simply changed from CCCP to RA. Aeroflot's paint scheme (including titles) is still recognisable, although this Tu-154M is a member of ROSSIYA's large fleet.

Right: UK-86569 is a member of the Uzbekistan Airways fleet, but operates on behalf of the government. Unlike the other Il-62s in the fleet UK-86569 is not a former Aeroflot or Interflug aircraft. It was delivered directly to Uzbekistan as one of the last Il-62Ms to be built. The Uzbeks appeared quite cautious as they brought their own guard to Zürich.

Big business

Above: Netherland's Royal Flight Fokker 28-1000 was photographed approaching Zürich. The registration PH-PBX was chosen because of the Queen's name, Beatrix. The aircraft is painted in the colours of the Royal family. In 1996 the aircraft was replaced by a Fokker 70 (PH-KBX). PH-PBX now flies as PK-RJW for Rajawali Air based in Jakarta, Indonesia.

Below: Until 1995 the Swiss bizjet company Aeroleasing operated DC-9-14 HB-IEF with HB-IFA (Swissair's first DC-9 in 1965). The spacious interior is equipped with 85 passenger seats. HB-IEF is now registered XA-SYQ and serves in Aerocalifornia's fleet, based in La Paz, Mexico.

Opposite above: The Fokker 28-1000 of Seabeco Trading in the old . . .

Opposite below: . . . and in the new paint scheme which was adopted in 1992. Originally designed as an airliner, the F28 operates worldwide as a bizjet. One of the reasons for its popularity is its excellent handling characteristics which make the aircraft easy to fly. In 1995 VR-BNC was sold to Peregrine Air Service in British Columbia, Canada.

Below: Although the Boeing 707's heyday in airline service has come to an end, the forty-year-old design is very popular as a 'king-size' bizjet. The interior of such an aircraft can be transformed into a four-room apartment – there is no limit. Only turbulence reminds passengers they are in the air. Kalair USA Corp's, N707KS is equipped with hush kits to make landings possible at noise-restricted airports. The registration N707KS was once carried by another Boeing 707, which is now registered N707SK.

Opposite above: When sheiks go shopping they usually need a lot of storage space! HZ-KA7 is a BAC 1-11/492 and is owned by Sheik Kamal Adham. This aircraft, c/n 260, is one of the last British-built BAC 1-11s. The Series 400 was developed especially for the US market to comply with the FAA requirements. As with most of today's flying BAC 1-11s the Rolls-Royce Spey engines are equipped with hush kits.

Opposite below: Rainbow colours are the trademark of Ashmawi Aviation based in Jeddah, Saudi Arabia. Mohammed Ashmawi owns many aircraft adorned with the same paint scheme, including a MU-2, Jetstar and a Sabreliner. Although the aircraft operate from Saudi Arabia, some aircraft carry Cayman Islands registrations. VR-CMI, a BAC 1-11/212, was spotted in 1992 during a short visit to Zürich.

Below: In 1987 the United States Central Intelligence Service (CIA) operated this Boeing 737-200 from Rhein-Main Air Base, Germany. Neither mission nor identity are clear. N99890 is probably military c/n 72-0286, a T-43A from the US Air Force inventory. The aircraft reappeared years later in the civil register as N5177C, flying with EG & G Special projects Inc, a contract company flying for federal organisations.

Above: A few seconds of sunshine were enough to photograph Sheik Mustafa's Boeing 737-2K5, HZ-MIS. Before the aircraft was converted to a 'flying penthouse' it was in airline service in Germany.

Above: Boeing 757-225 TP-01 is the largest aircraft in Mexico's government fleet. Named *Presidente Juarez*, the Boeing was factory-new when it arrived in Mexico in 1987. Despite being a member of the *Fuerza Aerea Mexicana* the civilian registration, XC-UJM, is carried on the fuselage. For international flights, the latter registration is used to avoid diplomatic complications. The Boeing 757 has now been re-registered XC-CBD.

Flying the generals: Military bizjets

Above: CM-02 is one of two Falcon 20Es used for VIP flights by the Belgian Air Force. The Falcon 20E is not equipped with thrust reversers but for short-field operations a drag chute is available in the tailcone. CM-02 was visiting Zürich Airport in February 1994. Note the Mirage-style cover for the AOA (Angle of Attack) probe and the pitot tubes.

Below: Several Falcon 20s serve with test units or VIP transport squadrons in the *Armée de l'Air*, where they are known as Mystère 20s. This sleek aircraft flew General Brun to Kauhava Air Base in Finland. The commander-in-chief of French Air Force Training Command visited the Finnish Air Force Academy in June 1995.

Left: The Swiss Air Force Falcon 50 was awaiting take-off clearance on the Emmen Air Base runway. When photographed in June 1996, T-783 still wore the typical ALG-style cheatlines of Aeroleasing SA, Geneva. The Swiss Air Force bought the aircraft, formerly registered HB-IEP, from Aeroleasing in order to replace one of its two Learjet 35s.

Below: Citation V TR.20-01 is one of 403 *Escadrón's* camera platforms. It was photographed at its home base in Cuatro Vientos, Madrid, in April 1994. Together with a second Citation and some CASA 212s it fulfils the photographic and survey tasks of the *Fuerza Aerea Española*. The right-hand camera pod is clearly visible in front of the wing root.
(*Uli Seibicke*)

Above: Citation V 0233 was photographed holding short of runway 28, awaiting a post maintenance test flight. The Pakistan Army pilots had already started checking the aircraft systems on the taxiway, and had found the thrust reversers to be working satisfactorily. This rarely seen Citation visited Zürich-Kloten in October 1994 for maintenance with Jet Aviation AG.

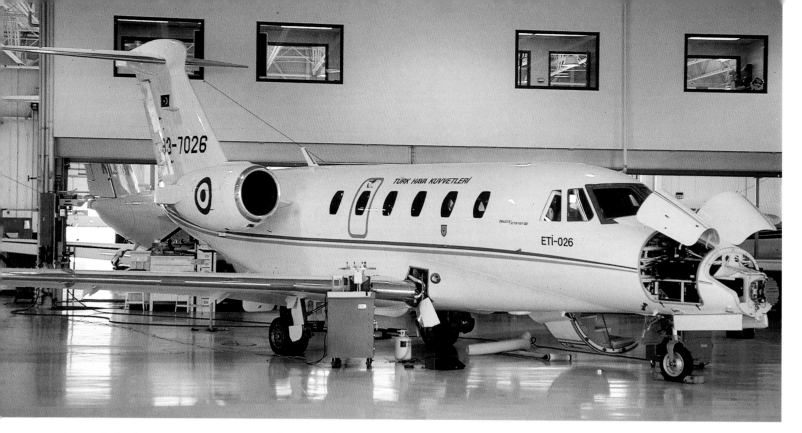

Above: Only four Cessna 650s entered service with military operators. Turkey bought two Citation VIIs and Chile bought two Citation IIIs but have already lost one. *Türk Hava Kuvvetleri's* 93-7026, c/n 650-7026, is based at Ankara-Etimesgut and was delivered in 1993. It was photographed in June 1994 during a visit to Cessna's service centre in Wichita, Kansas.

Below: Based on the Beech 400A, the T-1A Jayhawk is a pilot trainer for future transport and tanker pilots. It has a different fuel system with single point pressure refuelling, fewer cabin windows, reinforced windscreen protection against birdstrikes and a strengthened structure to handle more landings and increased low level flight stresses.

One instructor and two students arrived with 083 at Wichita on 11 June 1994. Wichita Mid-Continent Airport is often visited by fuel-stopping Jayhawks, with one student flying from Reese AFB to Wichita and the second one flying the return journey.

Above: T-782 is a second-hand Learjet 35A bought from Swiss Air Ambulance. Many Learjets fly in air forces worldwide. The US Air Force alone operates 84 Learjets. They are all Learjet 35As like this one.

Below: One of seven Challengers operated by *Flugbereitschaftsstaffel* in Cologne-Bonn, 06 was photographed in July 1996 in old-style markings with a small flag, small *Luftwaffe* title and a wide blue fuselage stripe. Other Challengers have already changed their outfits into more visible presentations.

Above: Originally designed as a short-range city hopper for a maximum of forty passengers, the VFW 614's first flight was on 14 July 1971 in Bremen. Despite utilising many new ideas, such as using carbon fibre-reinforced plastic for the landing gear doors and mounting the engines on top of the wings, the VFW 614 did not find much success with civilian customers. In 1995 three VFW 614s still flew in an executive transport role for the *Luftwaffe*, often used by the German Government.

Left: In November 1986 a C-140B Jetstar was photographed on final approach to Ramstein Air Base, Germany, shortly before its successor, the Gulfstream III, entered service. This Jetstar, 62-4200, was one of the first bizjets in military service, and was powered by four Pratt & Whitney JT12A-6A engines. Later versions of the Jetstar used four Garrett TFE731 engines and relocated long-range tanks.

Below: Whilst most European-based Sabreliners were painted white and grey and flown as utility aircraft in airlift squadrons, 62-4453 was painted in green camouflage and flew as a navigation aid calibration aircraft. It arrived at Wiesbaden, Germany, in 1972, moved to Rhein-Main AB in Frankfurt in 1976, and was operated by a Facility Checking Squadron until 1990. This CT-39A Sabreliner was used to check ILS (Instrument Landing System) installations on US military bases. During calibration flights, the Sabreliner performed ILS approaches, whilst avionics specialists monitored the ground signals with cabin-mounted Collins avionics. The USAF had operated Sabreliners in Europe since 1962, but on 10 December 1990 62-4453 was the last USAF Sabreliner to leave Europe.

Below: This is one of only two KC-135Es used by US Air Force active duty units. In contrast, over 160 are operated by the Air National Guard and Air Force Reserve units as air-to-air refuelling tankers. The former Strategic Command Commander-in-Chief's aircraft conducted a flight from Omaha, Nebraska, to Zürich-Kloten, arriving on 2 February 1996. It also stopped at Washington DC en route to pick up some VIPs.

Opposite above: In September 1995 Richard Holbrooke from the US State Department arrived in Geneva in this Gulfstream IV in order to lead the Peace Negotiations for former Yugoslavia. Normally based near Washington DC, this aircraft is designated as a C-20G. US-based VIP aircraft display the national insignia on the engine cowling, whilst USAF VIP aircraft based in Europe only display the national flag on the tail. Clearly, c/n 90-0300 is an exceptional case. The high frequency antenna on the tail is standard on newer military C-20s like this one, but there are also older models with retrofitted antennas.

Opposite below: Designated as Tp 102 in the Swedish Air Force, this aircraft can easily be identified as a Gulfstream IV. Grey-brown camouflaged 102001 was the first of three Swedish Gulfstreams.

Above: This visitor was photographed in February 1992 in holding bay 16, far away from the terminals of Zürich-Kloten Airport. It is Pakistan's presidential Boeing 707-351C, based in Islamabad. Notice the Krueger flaps beneath the wing leading edge.

Below: Usually a white star on a blue rudder is used to mark military aircraft owned by the *Fuerza Aerea de Chile*. However, some executive jets of *Grupo de Aviacion* No 10 use the whole tail to identify their nationality, like 901 a VIP Boeing 707-321B, c/n 19374, photographed during a state visit to Switzerland on 16 March 1995.

Above: President Carlos Menem's favourite airline, the *Fuerza Aerea Argentina*, operates T-01, a Boeing 757-23A, with Republica Argentina titles. The 1992-built aircraft, photographed in February 1993, replaced a much smaller Fokker 28-1000.

Below: A T-43A designated Boeing 737-253 of US Air Force 58th Military Airlift Squadron was photographed in March 1991. The Ramstein-based squadron uses a mixed bizjet fleet to provide executive transport for government and military VIPs in Europe. A similar-looking T-43 from the same unit occupied the newspaper headlines when US Commerce secretary Ron Brown and several leading US businessmen were involved in a fatal crash in April 1996 near Dubrovnik, Croatia.

Below: Even with the emergency exits removed this Czech Republic Tu-134A was still hot. The Tupolev joined the static display on a hot open day in Dijon, France, on 28 June 1992.

Opposite above: A US Navy aircraft belonging to the training squadron VT-86 was photographed parked at the Mid-Continent Airport in Wichita, Kansas. N310NT, a T-39N, arrived from a navigation training flight on 30 January 1997. The Sabreliner Corporation based in Chesterfield, Missouri, bought this Sabre 40, c/n 282-77, from a civilian customer, then overhauled and converted it to T-39N standard to fulfil a US Navy order.

Opposite below: 339-WN is one of the rarely seen Falcon 20SNAs flown by the *Armée de l'Air*. The aircraft was photographed during the 1992 Open day at Luxeuil, France. *Fil d'Ariane* carries a strange-looking nose – it is the radome of the Mirage F1, an example of which is standing in the background. In combination with the Mirage instruments on the cockpit's starboard side, the Falcon helps to instruct fighter pilots in complex radar systems. In the register c/n 451 is also found with the civilian registration F-UKJC, which is not painted on the aircraft.

Work in progress

Above: HB-VIK, the BAe 125-800B operated by Swiss Air Ambulance, was photographed a few minutes after paintstripping had been completed by Jet Aviation Zürich. The flight controls can be seen in the foreground. Because of the aggressive fluid used, all plastic parts such as the radome, the windows and the top of the tailfin have to be covered or removed. The leading edges are also very sensitive and are therefore removed as well.

Opposite above: It's incredible that someone can assemble all these parts to form a functional Citation I cockpit, but it is a typical task for an avionics technician. All connectors, instrument panels and wire bundles are labelled and removal and installation instructions are outlined in the technical manuals. Nevertheless, individual records of the sequence of removal are more than helpful to reinstall all parts. Each reinstalled part will be tested before the aircraft can be released into service.

Opposite below: This covered Citation III has just been repainted on the tailsection. Even relatively small paint jobs are time-consuming. Aircraft systems are extremely sensitive and pollution from paint grinding and paint spraying should be avoided. Engine inlets, air scoops, sensors and windows are therefore covered with masking tape.

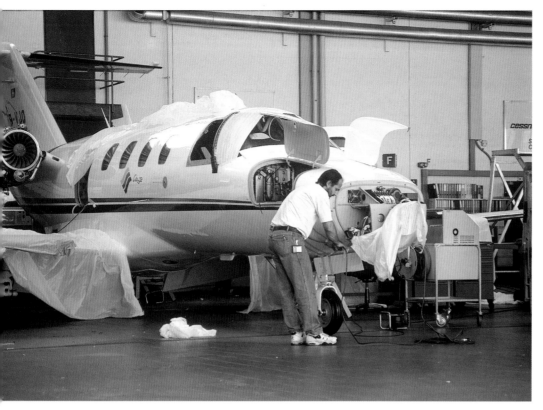

Left: Here is another Citation undergoing maintenance. This CitationJet will be prepared for functional testing of the pitot/static system. A closer look at the right-hand cockpit side window reveals that the window panel has been replaced.

Below: This is a typical scene during the World Economic Forum which takes place every winter in Switzerland. Bizjets of all countries, including civilian and military, and 'vintage' jets and brand-new demonstrators, fill Zürich Airport.